BEHIND THE BRAND

NINTENDO

BY PAIGE V. POLINSKY

BLASTOFF!
DISCOVERY

BELLWETHER MEDIA • MINNEAPOLIS, MN

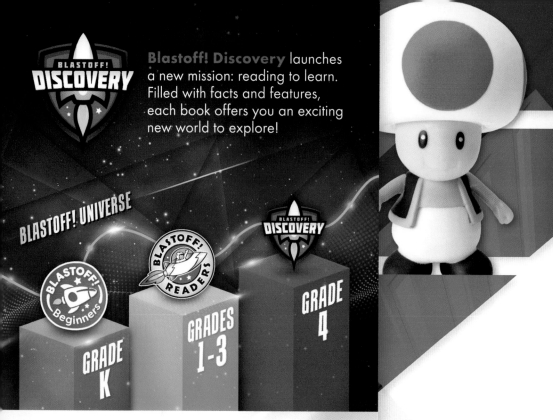

Blastoff! Discovery launches a new mission: reading to learn. Filled with facts and features, each book offers you an exciting new world to explore!

This edition first published in 2023 by Bellwether Media, Inc.

Library of Congress Cataloging-in-Publication Data

Names: Polinsky, Paige V., author.
Title: Nintendo / by Paige V. Polinsky.
Description: Minneapolis, MN : Bellwether Media, 2023. | Series: Blastoff! discovery.
Behind the brand | Includes bibliographical references and index. | Audience:
Ages 7-13 | Audience: Grades 4-6 | Summary: "Engaging images accompany
information about Nintendo. The combination of high-interest subject matter and
narrative text is intended for students in grades 3 through 8"– Provided by publisher.
Identifiers: LCCN 2022049467 (print) | LCCN 2022049468 (ebook) |
ISBN 9798886871432 (library binding) | ISBN 9798886872095 (paperback) |
ISBN 9798886872699 (ebook)
Subjects: LCSH: Nintendo video games–Juvenile literature.
Classification: LCC GV1469.32 .P65 2023 (print) | LCC GV1469.32 (ebook) |
DDC 794.8–dc23/eng/20221017
LC record available at https://lccn.loc.gov/2022049467
LC ebook record available at https://lccn.loc.gov/2022049468

Editor: Betsy Rathburn   Designer: Andrea Schneider

Printed in the United States of America, North Mankato, MN.

TABLE OF CONTENTS

RAINBOW RACE!

A family is playing on their Nintendo Switch. They are competing for the Special Cup in *Mario Kart 8 Deluxe*! They race along a giant beanstalk in the clouds. They zoom through desert canyons and a lava-filled castle.

The final course is Rainbow Road. At the starting line, the players charge their turbo boosts. The race is on! Peach pulls ahead quickly. But Toad and Donkey Kong are close behind. They drift around corners and soar off ramps. It is a close race. But Toad hits Peach with a red shell. Toad takes the lead and finishes first!

REXA

Rainbow
Explorati
Agency

– – TOAD

NINTENDO SWITCH

PEACH

LEVELING UP

MARIO

POKÉMON TOYS

Nintendo is one of the most popular gaming companies of all time! Some of its creations, such as the Mario and Pokémon series, are among the world's best-selling games. The company's **consoles** are also top sellers. Nintendo makes toys, movies, and theme parks, too.

Nintendo's **headquarters** is in Kyoto, Japan. Artist Fusajiro Yamauchi started the company on September 23, 1889. He sold handmade playing cards called *hanafuda*. They featured art instead of numbers. The cards were very popular.

NINTENDO HEADQUARTERS

KYOTO, JAPAN

ASIA

In 1949, Fusajiro's great-grandson, Hiroshi Yamauchi, became president of Nintendo. Hiroshi wanted Nintendo to grow. It soon became the first company to sell plastic playing cards in Japan. Nintendo even partnered with Disney to sell sets featuring Disney characters. This helped boost sales. But the card **industry** was small. Hiroshi wanted more.

HIROSHI YAMAUCHI

ULTRA HAND

Nintendo soon got involved in other industries, including taxis and food. None were successful. The company's card sales began to slow. Hiroshi decided to try making toys. In 1966, the Ultra Hand was released. Nintendo's first toy was a success!

DONKEY KONG
ARCADE GAMES

EARLY
GAME & WATCH

In the 1960s, electronic games were growing in popularity. Nintendo created many through the 1970s. In 1980, the company released the first Game & Watch. These handheld games let people play on the go!

In 1981, Nintendo released *Donkey Kong* for **arcades**. Created by Shigeru Miyamoto, this popular **platform game** was the first game to feature Mario. He was the first video game character who could jump! Two years later, Nintendo released the Famicom. People could now play *Donkey Kong* and other games at home!

SHIGERU MIYAMOTO

BORN November 16, 1952, in Sonobe, Japan

ROLE Nintendo game designer, producer, and director

ACCOMPLISHMENTS

Worked on *Donkey Kong*, *Super Mario Bros.*, *The Legend of Zelda*, and many other games

Nintendo redesigned the Famicom and introduced it in the United States in 1985. It was now called the Nintendo Entertainment System, or NES. The NES was released with *Super Mario Bros.* This game sent *Donkey Kong*'s Mario on a new adventure. By the end of 1986, it was a bestseller!

NINTENDO
ENTERTAINMENT
SYSTEM

000300

LINK IN
THE LEGEND OF ZELDA

SUPER MARIO BROS.

More games followed. In 1987, *The Legend of Zelda* was released in the U.S. The game followed Link on an adventure to save a princess. Players solved puzzles and fought enemies. The game was the first to let players save their progress and pick up where they left off!

SUPER SMASH HITS

CARTRIDGES

Nintendo GAME BOY™

DOT MATRIX WITH STEREO SOUND

BATTERY

SELECT   START

SUPER NINTENDO

GAME BOY

Nintendo continued its focus on video games. In 1989, the Game Boy launched. Its low price and long battery life crushed competition. People used **cartridges** to play different games on the go! *Tetris* and *Super Mario Land* were early hits. In 1998, *Pokémon Red* and *Blue* were released in North America. They were huge sellers!

The 1990s also brought new home consoles from Nintendo. In 1991, the Super Nintendo was released in the U.S. It had improved **graphics** and speeds. The cartridges had more space, so games could be more complex. *Super Mario World* was a favorite!

OUT OF THIS WORLD

In 1993, the Game Boy went to space! Russian astronaut Aleksandr Serebrov brought one to the MIR Space Station to play *Tetris*.

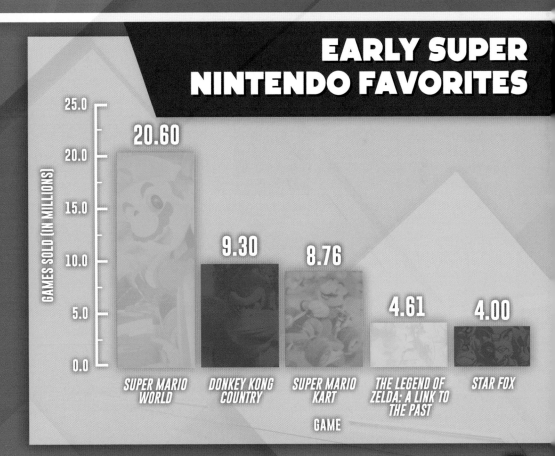

EARLY SUPER NINTENDO FAVORITES

GAMES SOLD (IN MILLIONS)

20.60 — SUPER MARIO WORLD
9.30 — DONKEY KONG COUNTRY
8.76 — SUPER MARIO KART
4.61 — THE LEGEND OF ZELDA: A LINK TO THE PAST
4.00 — STAR FOX

GAME

In 1996, Nintendo launched the Nintendo 64. *Super Mario 64* was the star title. Its **3D** graphics changed gaming forever. Players could spin the camera and move Mario in any direction! In the following years, more favorites such as *The Legend of Zelda: Ocarina of Time* and *Super Smash Bros.* were released.

NINTENDO TIMELINE

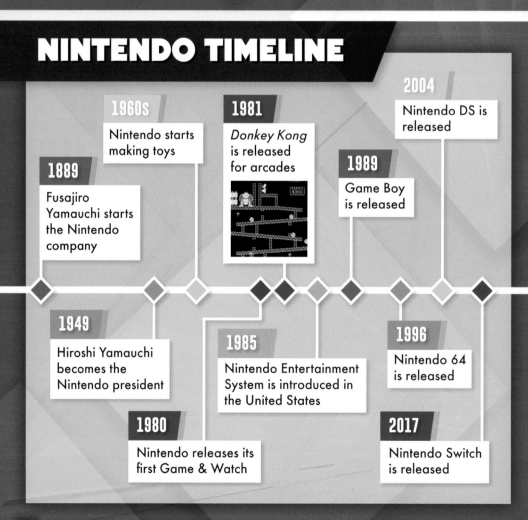

2004
Nintendo DS is released

1960s
Nintendo starts making toys

1981
Donkey Kong is released for arcades

1889
Fusajiro Yamauchi starts the Nintendo company

1989
Game Boy is released

1949
Hiroshi Yamauchi becomes the Nintendo president

1985
Nintendo Entertainment System is introduced in the United States

1996
Nintendo 64 is released

1980
Nintendo releases its first Game & Watch

2017
Nintendo Switch is released

GAMECUBE

GAME BOY ADVANCE

Nintendo's next home console was the GameCube, released in 2001. Sales were low. The handheld Game Boy Advance also released that year. Three years later, the Nintendo DS was released. To this day, it remains the world's best-selling handheld console!

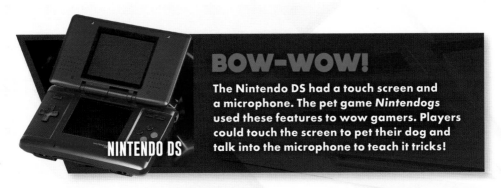

NINTENDO DS

BOW-WOW!

The Nintendo DS had a touch screen and a microphone. The pet game *Nintendogs* used these features to wow gamers. Players could touch the screen to pet their dog and talk into the microphone to teach it tricks!

17

POKÉMON GO

In July 2016, developer Niantic worked with Nintendo to create an AR mobile game. *Pokémon GO* was an instant hit! It lets players catch, train, and battle Pokémon in real-world locations!

WII WIRELESS MOTION CONTROL

In 2006, Nintendo replaced the GameCube with the Wii. This home console featured wireless **motion control**. People loved using it to play *Wii Sports*. Other family-friendly titles also proved popular. The Wii quickly became Nintendo's top home console. More than 100 million were sold over time!

In 2011, the Nintendo 3DS became the first handheld console offering a 3D display and **augmented reality** (AR). The Wii U came out the following year. It featured Nintendo's best graphics yet. It was not very popular. But it had many hit games, such as *Splatoon*.

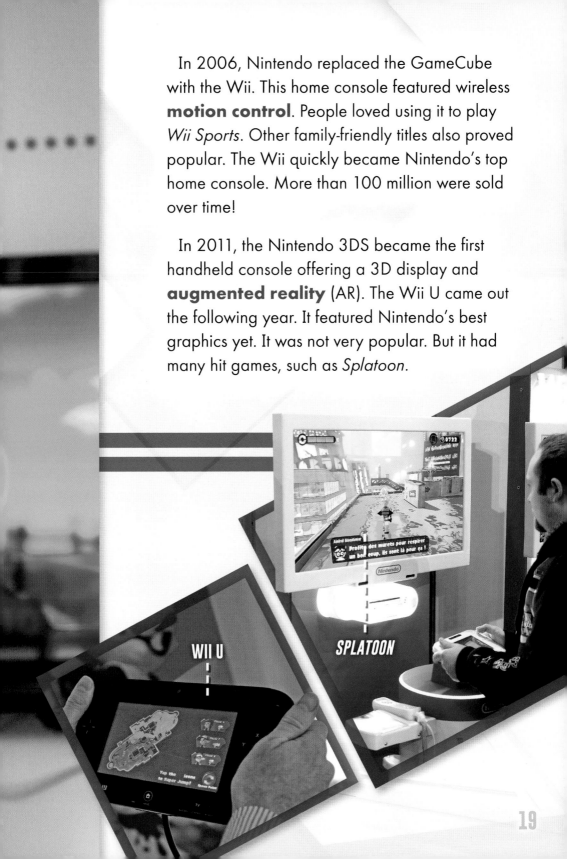

WII U

SPLATOON

SUPER MARIO RUN

SUPER MARIO ODYSSEY ON A NINTENDO SWITCH

Nintendo revealed *Super Mario Run* in December 2016. The mobile game launched in 150 countries. In four days, it hit 40 million downloads! The Nintendo Switch came out in 2017. It could be played like a handheld system or a home console. It offered gamers the best of both worlds!

Mario Kart 8 Deluxe set sales records on the Nintendo Switch. *The Legend of Zelda: Breath of the Wild* and *Super Mario Odyssey* featured huge, open areas. *Splatoon 2* let players battle online. The Switch overtook the Wii as Nintendo's best-selling home console!

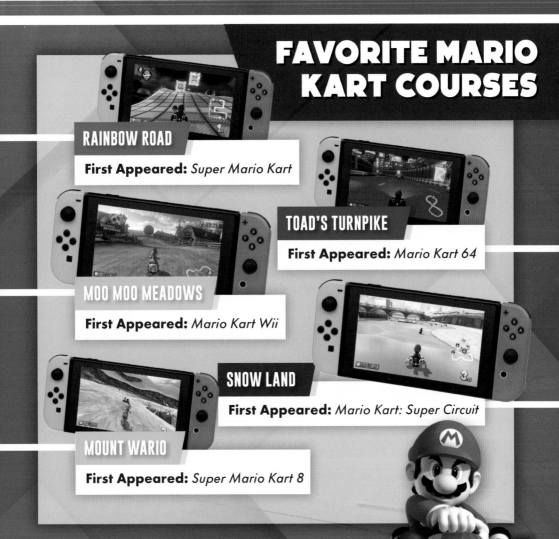

FAVORITE MARIO KART COURSES

RAINBOW ROAD
First Appeared: *Super Mario Kart*

TOAD'S TURNPIKE
First Appeared: *Mario Kart 64*

MOO MOO MEADOWS
First Appeared: *Mario Kart Wii*

SNOW LAND
First Appeared: *Mario Kart: Super Circuit*

MOUNT WARIO
First Appeared: *Super Mario Kart 8*

More Switch success followed. In 2018, *Super Smash Bros. Ultimate* was a smash hit. Sales passed 5 million in its first week! The following year brought hits like the exercise game *Ring Fit Adventure*. *Animal Crossing: New Horizons* released in 2020. It let players catch insects, go fishing, and decorate islands!

NINTENDO SWITCH FAVORITES

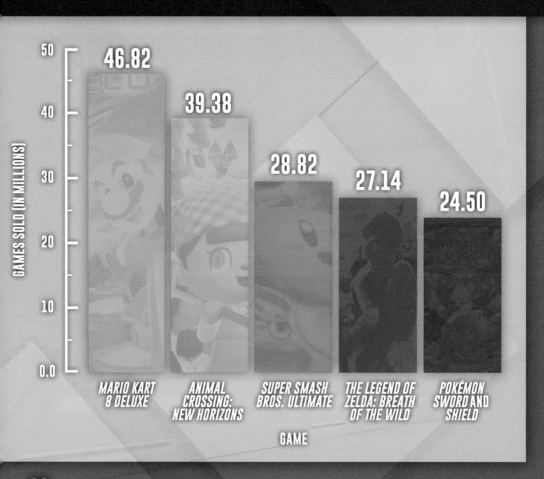

GAMES SOLD (IN MILLIONS)

Game	Games Sold (in millions)
MARIO KART 8 DELUXE	46.82
ANIMAL CROSSING: NEW HORIZONS	39.38
SUPER SMASH BROS. ULTIMATE	28.82
THE LEGEND OF ZELDA: BREATH OF THE WILD	27.14
POKÉMON SWORD AND SHIELD	24.50

GAME

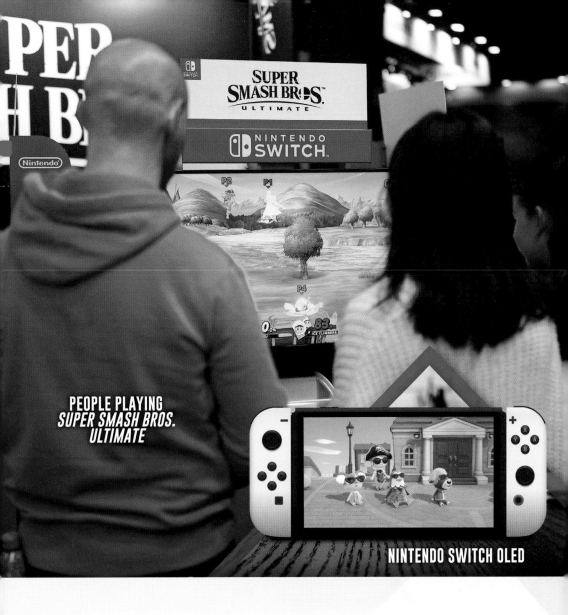

SUPER SMASH BROS. ULTIMATE

NINTENDO SWITCH

PEOPLE PLAYING SUPER SMASH BROS. ULTIMATE

NINTENDO SWITCH OLED

The Nintendo Switch OLED launched in 2021. It features an improved kickstand and a bigger, better screen. New games also add fun. *Pokémon Scarlet* and *Violet* released in 2022. The following year, *The Legend of Zelda: Tears of the Kingdom* came out. Nintendo also released a new movie, *The Super Mario Bros. Movie,* in 2023. Nintendo fans always have something to look forward to!

NINTENDO GIVES BACK

PLAYING A NINTENDO WII AT A STARLIGHT CHILDREN'S FOUNDATION EVENT

Nintendo makes a difference in the world! The company works with Starlight Children's **Foundation** to help kids living with illnesses. In 2020, they gave 350 gaming stations for kids to play in hospitals.

Nintendo has also given computers to families who do not have one at home. During the COVID-19 **pandemic** this helped students stay connected to their teachers and classmates. In 2021, the company gave Nintendo Switch consoles to help teach elderly people about technology. Nintendo welcomes fans of all ages!

GIVING BACK

MORE THAN 7,200 GAMING STATIONS
GIVEN TO HOSPITALS

350 GAMING STATIONS
GIVEN TO HOSPITALS IN 2020

130 LAPTOPS
GIVEN TO HELP KIDS IN 2021

SUPER NINTENDO WORLD
UNIVERSAL STUDIOS JAPAN

SUPER NINTENDO WORLD

In 2021, Super Nintendo World opened at Universal Studios Japan. The theme park features Nintendo-themed rides, foods, and more!

Nintendo fans use their favorite games to give to **charities**, too. **Speedrunning** events such as Games Done Quick are popular. Players finish games as quickly as possible to raise money for charity. Summer Games Done Quick 2022 raised over $3 million for Doctors Without Borders!

Zeldathon is another popular charity event. Every game from the Legend of Zelda series is finished over only a few days. Players complete fun challenges to encourage viewers to give money to charity. They may play upside-down or wear a costume. The Nintendo community encourages people to do good!

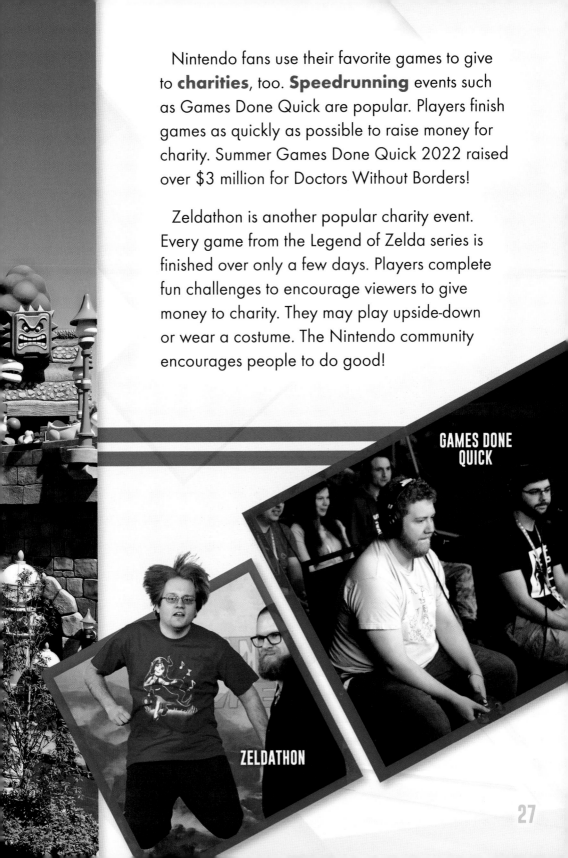

GAMES DONE QUICK

ZELDATHON

27

ZELDA COSPLAYER

GAMING CONVENTION

Conventions also bring Nintendo fans together.
Gamers can browse booths that sell Nintendo items,
play in arcades, meet special guests, and more.
Many choose to **cosplay** during these events.
They bring their favorite Nintendo characters to life!

Many conventions host exciting **esports** events. Super Smash Con began in 2015. Players play Super Smash Bros. games to compete for prizes. In 2021, Nintendo announced North America's first official Super Smash Bros. championship. It features a $100,000 prize pool. Nintendo brings fun to fans around the world!

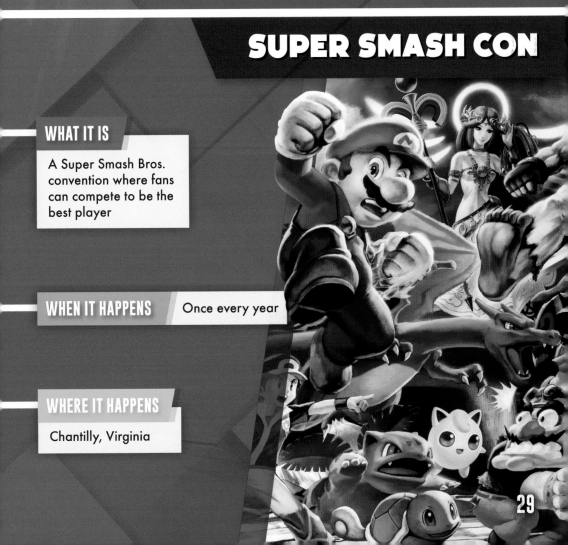

SUPER SMASH CON

WHAT IT IS

A Super Smash Bros. convention where fans can compete to be the best player

WHEN IT HAPPENS Once every year

WHERE IT HAPPENS

Chantilly, Virginia

GLOSSARY

3D—showing length, height, and depth

arcades—places where people can play coin-operated games

augmented reality—a technology that uses cameras to place an image on top of the real-world surroundings

cartridges—small electronic devices that contain video game software; cartridges are put into consoles to play video games.

charities—organizations that help others in need

consoles—electronic devices for playing video games

conventions—events where fans of a subject meet

cosplay—to dress up as a character from a movie, book, or video game

esports—multiplayer video games played in competitions

foundation—an organization that gives money to people or groups in need

graphics—art such as illustrations or designs

headquarters—a company's main office

industry—businesses that provide a certain product or service

motion control—a technology that lets people control something using their own movements

pandemic—an outbreak of a disease over a whole country or the world

platform game—a game in which characters jump on platforms to get to new places

speedrunning—playing a game as quickly as possible in order to finish within a certain amount of time

TO LEARN MORE

AT THE LIBRARY

Bolte, Mari. *Super Mario*. Chicago, Ill.: Norwood House Press, 2022.

Castro, Rachel. *Shigeru Miyamoto*. Chicago, Ill.: Norwood House Press, 2020.

Thomas, Rachel L. *Nintendo Innovator: Hiroshi Yamauchi*. Minneapolis, Minn.: Abdo Publishing, 2019.

ON THE WEB

FACTSURFER

Factsurfer.com gives you a safe, fun way to find more information.

1. Go to www.factsurfer.com.

2. Enter "Nintendo" into the search box and click 🔍.

3. Select your book cover to see a list of related content.

INDEX